Earth in Action

Floods

by Matt Doeden

Consulting Editor: Gail Saunders-Smith, PhD

Consultant: Susan L. Cutter, PhD
Carolina Distinguished Professor and Director,
Hazards & Vulnerability Research Institute
Department of Geography, University of South Carolina

CAPSTONE PRESS
a capstone imprint

Pebble Plus is published by Capstone Press,
151 Good Counsel Drive, P.O. Box 669, Mankato, Minnesota 56002.
www.capstonepress.com

092009
005618CGS10

Library of Congress Cataloging-in-Publication Data
Doeden, Matt.
    Floods / by Matt Doeden.
       p. cm. — (Pebble plus. Earth in action)
    Summary: "Describes floods, how they occur, and ways to stay safe during a flood" — Provided by publisher.
    Includes bibliographical references and index.
    ISBN 978-1-4296-4720-5 (library binding)
    1. Floods — Juvenile literature. I. Title. II. Series: Pebble plus. Earth in action.
GB1399.D64 2010
551.48'9 — dc22   2009036868

Editorial Credits
Erika L. Shores, editor; Heidi Thompson, designer; Jo Miller, media researcher; Eric Mankse, production specialist

Photo Credits
FEMA News Photo/Jocelyn Augustino, 5, 7; Melissa Ann Janssen, 19
Getty Images Inc./Chris Graythen, 13; Joe Raedle, 21; Matt Cardy, 17; Scott Olson, cover, 9
Shutterstock/Four Oaks, 1, 11; Jerry Horbert, 15

Note to Parents and Teachers

The Earth in Action set supports national science standards related to earth science. This book
describes and illustrates floods. The images support early readers in understanding the text. The
repetition of words and phrases helps early readers learn new words. This book also introduces
early readers to subject-specific vocabulary words, which are defined in the Glossary section.
Early readers may need assistance to read some words and to use the Table of Contents,
Glossary, Read More, Internet Sites, and Index sections of the book.

Table of Contents

What Is a Flood?

Floods happen when water covers places it usually doesn't. Floods are the most common natural disaster in the United States.

What Causes Floods?

Heavy rain causes flash floods.
The ground cannot soak up
all the rainwater.
Floods also happen when
a levee or a dam breaks.

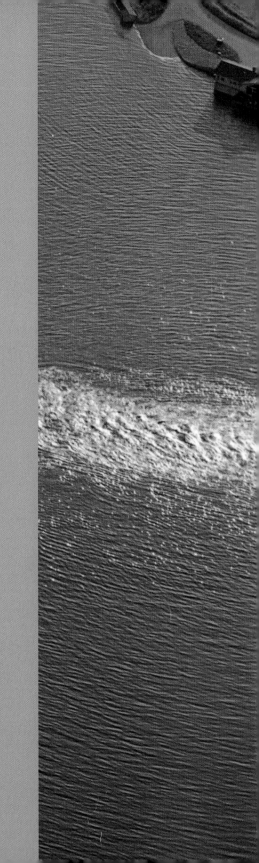

Rain or melting snow

can make rivers overflow.

Other times hurricanes

blow ocean water onto land.

Dangers of Floods

Floods are dangerous.

Moving water can sweep away

people and cars.

Floods can wash away

roads and bridges.

Floods often damage homes
and buildings.

Wet wood rots inside walls.

Dangerous mold grows.

Staying Safe

People should move to
high ground during a flood.
They should never drive
on flooded roads.

Dirty flood waters

can spread diseases.

During floods, people should

drink and cook

with bottled water.

Scientists use radar and other tools to predict floods. They send out flood warnings. Warnings tell people an area is in danger of flooding.

People can prepare for floods.

They pile sandbags to keep

water away from buildings.

Sometimes people leave their

homes until the flood is over.

Glossary

flash flood — a flood that happens with little or no warning, often during periods of heavy rainfall

flood warning — an official announcement that an area is in immediate danger of flooding

high ground — an area that lies above flood waters

hurricane — a very large storm with high winds and rain; hurricanes form over warm ocean water.

levee — a slope or barrier, usually made of earth, that stops flood waters

mold — a fungus that often grows on damp objects; some types of mold can be harmful to people.

predict — to make an informed guess that something will happen

radar — a weather tool that sends out microwaves to determine a storm's size, strength, and movement

sandbag — a bag filled with sand that, when stacked with other bags, can hold back flood waters for a short period of time.

Read More

Chambers, Catherine. *Flood.* Wild Weather. Chicago: Heinemann Library, 2007.

Ganeri, Anita. *Flood!* Nature's Fury. North Mankato, Minn.: Arcturus Pub., 2006.

Thomas, Rick. *Rising Waters: A Book about Floods.* Amazing Science. Minneapolis: Picture Window Books, 2005.

Internet Sites

FactHound offers a safe, fun way to find Internet sites related to this book. All of the sites on FactHound have been researched by our staff.

Here's all you do:
Visit *www.facthound.com*

FactHound will fetch the best sites for you!

Index

Word Count: 171

Grade: 1

Early-Intervention Level: 16